HAWAII

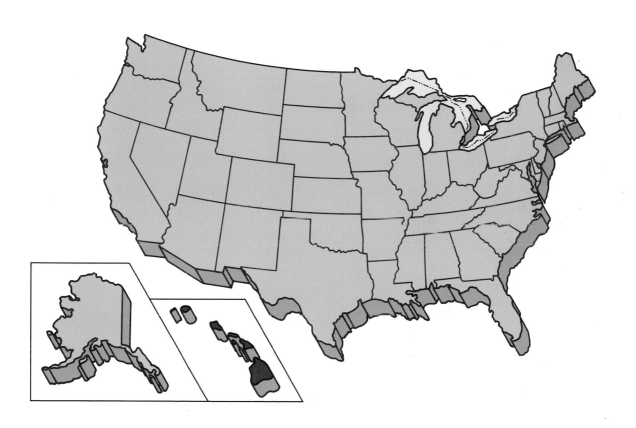

HAWAII

Joyce Johnston

 Lerner Publications Company

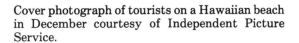

Cover photograph of tourists on a Hawaiian beach in December courtesy of Independent Picture Service.

The glossary on page 69 gives definitions of words shown in **bold type** in the text.

LIBRARY OF CONGRESS
CATALOGING-IN-PUBLICATION DATA
Johnston, Joyce.
   Hawaii / Joyce Johnston.
     p. cm. — (Hello U.S.A.)
   Includes index.
   ISBN 0-8225-2739-1 (lib. bdg.)
   1. Hawaii—Juvenile literature. I. Title.
II. Series.
DU623.25.J64 1994
919.69—dc20   93-46907
                  CIP
                  AC

Manufactured in the United States of America

1 2 3 4 5 6 - I/JR - 00 99 98 97 96 95

 This book is printed on acid-free, recyclable paper.

CONTENTS

Did You Know . . . ?

❑ Surfing was invented thousands of years ago by the Polynesian peoples who first settled Hawaii. They rode ocean waves on carved boards that weighed more than 150 pounds (68 kilograms) and measured up to 20 feet (6 meters) in length. Modern surfboards weigh about 12 pounds (5 kg) and are only 6 feet (2 m) long.

❑ Hawaii is the only state completely made up of islands. It is also the only state where you'll find coffee plantations and **tropical rain forests.**

❑ Mount Waialeale on Hawaii's Kauai Island is one of the wettest spots on earth. The 5,208-foot (1,587-m) mountain receives more than 400 inches (1,016 centimeters) of rain each year.

❏ Mauna Loa, on the island of Hawaii, is the world's largest volcano. From the ocean floor, Mauna Loa rises 31,784 feet (9,688 m)—but less than half of its height is actually above sea level.

❏ Every year about 1.5 million people view the remains of the USS *Arizona* at Pearl Harbor. The warship and its crew were bombed by Japan during a surprise raid on the naval base in 1941.

❏ In the 1960s, astronauts trained for moon voyages by walking on Mauna Loa's cooled and hardened lava fields, which resemble the surface of the moon.

A Trip
Around the State

Imagine leaving the West Coast of the United States on a ship. As the boat cruises toward the southwest, you scan the Pacific Ocean for land. Finally, on the fifth day at sea, islands appear in the distance. After traveling more than 2,400 miles (3,862 kilometers), the ship has reached Hawaii—the southernmost state in the United States.

A chain of 132 islands, Hawaii lies in the middle of the North Pacific Ocean. The chain stretches 1,523 miles (2,451 km) northwest from Hawaii Island, the state's largest island.

Hawaii is known for its volcanoes (above) **and sandy beaches** (facing page).

8

KAUAI

NIIHAU

The Hawaiian Islands began forming millions of years ago when magma (hot, liquid rock) oozed from deep within the earth onto the floor of the Pacific Ocean. The liquid cooled, leaving a layer of hardened, volcanic rock called **lava** on the ocean floor. Over the ages, more and more magma trickled from the earth, piling the layers of lava higher and higher.

While the magma oozed, the ocean floor crept very slowly toward the northwest. The movement pulled the first volcano away from the "hot spot," where the magma was seeping from inside the earth. A new volcano was then created above the hot spot. As these actions were repeated, and the ocean floor shifted, the magma eventually formed a string of volcanoes. One by one, the volcanoes rose above the waves, forming the Hawaiian Islands.

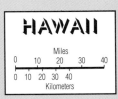

HAWAII

Miles

0   10   20   30   40

0 10 20 30 40

Kilometers

OAHU

HONOLULU

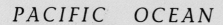
MOLOKAI

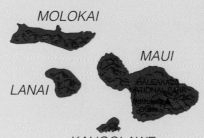
MAUI

LANAI

HALEAKALA
NATIONAL PARK

Haleakala
Crater

KAHOOLAWE

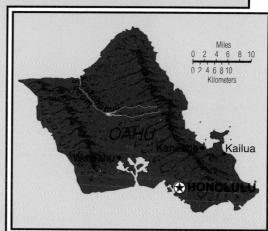

Miles
0 2 4 6 8 10

0 2 4 6 8 10
Kilometers

Koolau Range

Waianae Range

OAHU

Kaneohe •

Kailua

Wahiawa •

HONOLULU

HAWAII

Mauna Kea

Wailuku R.

Hilo

Mauna Loa

HAWAII
VOLCANOES
NATIONAL PARK

PACIFIC   OCEAN

Hawaii is divided into two groups of islands. The first group is made up of 124 small islands, which form the northwestern part of the chain. Wind and water have worn down these islands, leaving only pieces of volcanic rock and islands made of **coral**—or layers of limestone.

The second group consists of eight large islands. Maui and Kahoolawe islands lie northwest of Hawaii Island. Lanai and Molokai are next in the chain, followed by Oahu, Kauai, and Niihau.

Streams, ocean waves, and wind have shaped Hawaii's rugged, volcanic mountains. The highest peak in the state is Mauna Kea, an inactive volcano that rises 13,796 feet (4,205 m) near the center of

Colorful fish swim past an underwater coral formation.

On Kauai Island, cropland spreads out on both sides of the Hanalei River.

Hawaii Island. Two of the other volcanoes on Hawaii Island—Mauna Loa and Kilauea—still erupt from time to time.

Although Hawaii is mountainous, flatlands and lowlands spread over parts of the state. Hawaii's lowlands include the coastal plain of Molokai Island and a wide valley on Maui. On Oahu a broad **plateau** (flat highland) separates the Koolau and Waianae mountain ranges. Farmers raise livestock or plant sugarcane, pineapples, and other crops in these areas.

A rainbow of color streaks the bark of painted eucalyptus—one of the many trees found in Hawaii's tropical rain forests.

In general, temperatures on the islands are warm and remain fairly constant throughout the year. In the lowlands, temperatures average 77° F (25° C) in July and 71° F (22° C) in January. During the winter months, winds from the southwest bring hot, sticky air and storms—including hurricanes. Only on Hawaii's highest mountaintops are temperatures cold enough for snow.

Steady breezes known as the trade winds bring rainstorms that drop most of their moisture on the northeastern side of the islands. As much as 400 inches (1,016 cm) of rain fall each year in the state's mountain rain forests. But some valleys and lowlands on the southwestern side of the islands receive 10 inches (25 cm) or less of rain annually.

Only a few short rivers flow across the islands. The longest of these waterways are the Kaukonahua Stream on Oahu, the Wailuku River on Hawaii Island, and the Waimea River on Kauai.

14

Mauna Kea *(above),* **an inactive volcano, usually gets enough snow during the winter months for skiing. In a few of the state's dry spots, hikers are likely to spot a silversword plant** *(inset).*

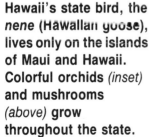

Hawaii's state bird, the *nene* (Hawaiian goose), lives only on the islands of Maui and Hawaii. Colorful orchids *(inset)* and mushrooms *(above)* grow throughout the state.

Hawaii's warm and humid climate makes the state a natural greenhouse, where many different kinds of plants thrive. Orchids, hibiscus, and other flowering plants that need a lot of moisture bloom on the rainy side of the islands. In the state's rain forests, some ferns reach 40 feet (12 m) in height, with stems as thick as tree trunks. Cactuses and other desert plants are found in drier areas.

Only two types of mammals—the hoary bat and the monk seal—are native to Hawaii. But the islands are known for their many birds and sea creatures. Birds such as honeycreepers, which are found only in Hawaii, inhabit the rain forests. Colorful fish darting among coral reefs, sea turtles paddling below the ocean waves, and humpback whales slapping the water with their tails are just a few of Hawaii's underwater treasures.

17

(Above) **Young Polynesian men studied for many years to learn how to build canoes. The biggest oceangoing canoes, used in warfare and for long-distance travel, could carry as many as 200 people.** *(Facing page)* **Polynesians placed offerings on rock carvings when asking special favors of their gods.**

Hawaii's Story

Hawaii is just one of many groups of islands in a vast region of the Pacific Ocean known as Polynesia. The people who have lived in this part of the world for thousands of years are called Polynesians. The name means "people of the many islands."

Ancient Polynesians were expert navigators. They explored immense stretches of ocean in sailboats, which they made by lashing two huge canoes together and raising a sail. The Polynesian sailors used the stars, clouds, ocean currents, and even seabirds to find their way from island to island.

In about A.D. 300, Polynesians from the Marquesas Islands loaded their canoes with seeds, food, and livestock. They sailed north, carrying their cargo as well as a few rats that had snuck onto the boats.

After traveling 2,000 miles (3,218 km), the sailors discovered a group of islands. They called the land Hawaiki, a name the Polynesians also used to refer to their ancient Asian homeland. The state of Hawaii takes its name from this word.

Hawaiian women made *tapa* cloth by beating tree bark into soft, pulpy strips that could be sewn together.

About 600 years later, another group of Polynesians sailed to Hawaii from the Pacific island of Tahiti. Both groups of ancient Hawaiians worshipped many gods. The islanders believed that their chiefs, or *alii*, were related to these gods.

Makaainana, or ordinary Hawaiians, performed everyday tasks. The men grew coconuts, sweet potatoes, bananas, and sugarcane. They also prepared *poi*, a pudding-like dish made from the taro plant. Some makaainana men collected colorful feathers for decorating the capes and helmets of the alii. Others chopped down *koa* trees and carved the logs into canoes. Women cared for children, tended gardens, and made clothing.

Pele's Volcano

Ancient Hawaiian religious beliefs were based on respect for the powers of nature. Many different gods represented these forces. Hawaiians worshipped some of their gods in the form of idols, or images, made of feathers, wood, stones, shells, and human hair. Trained storytellers told the tales of the gods' lives to a circle of listeners, who were forbidden to move once the sacred story had begun.

Among the most important Hawaiian gods were Ku (the god of war), Kane (the god of life), Lono (the god of the harvest), and Pele (the goddess of fire). Hawaiians believed that Pele lived at Kilauea volcano on the island of Hawaii. They thought she was responsible for Kilauea's lava flows and anything else related to heat and fire. Nowadays prayers to Pele are still said when a new *imu,* or underground oven, is built.

And park rangers at Hawaii Volcanoes National Park on the island of Hawaii receive packages every year from tourists who have taken volcanic rocks from Kilauea as souvenirs. These vacationers return the rocks to the park, claiming that bad luck followed them the minute they took the souvenirs from Pele's volcano.

Rules called *kapu* guided daily life. For example, makaainana could not let their shadows touch the shadow of an alii. Women were not allowed to eat certain foods or to share meals with men. The punishment for breaking kapu was usually death.

Until the late 1700s, the rest of the world didn't know that Hawaii existed. One night in 1778, two Hawaiian fishermen spotted what looked like two islands floating off the coast of Kauai Island. The men quickly paddled to shore to tell others what they had seen. In the

The *hula* was originally a form of worship performed only by highly trained men. According to Hawaiian beliefs, a god named Laka taught men how to do the hula.

Because Captain Cook landed during a festival that was sacred to Hawaiians, they thought he was a god and offered him gifts.

morning, people gathered on the beach. The floating islands were two large ships.

The ships carried Captain James Cook, a British officer, and his crew. Cook and his men were searching for the Northwest Passage, a water route thought to lead from Europe to Asia.

Although Cook did not stay in Hawaii for long, he and his crew returned later that year to collect food and water. The Hawaiians celebrated the return with parties and feasts that lasted for several weeks. But during their stay, the British ate most of the Hawaiians' food and unknowingly broke many kapu. When the British ships finally loft, the Hawaiians were glad to see their visitors go.

The explorers didn't get far. After a storm damaged their ships, the British returned to Hawaii for repairs. This time, the Hawaiians were not happy to see the sailors and threw rocks at the returning ships.

John Webber, an artist who traveled with Cook and his crew to record events, painted this picture of the captain's death.

The situation worsened when Hawaiian villagers stole a cutter (small supply boat) belonging to Captain Cook. To get the cutter back, Cook went ashore and tried to capture the local alii. Cook planned to hold the chief hostage until the boat was returned. In the fight that followed, Captain Cook and several Hawaiians were killed.

At the time of Cook's death, Hawaii was ruled by four alii. But in the 1780s, Kamehameha I— the ruling chief of Hawaii Island—fought for control of all the islands in a lengthy war. By 1810 Kamehameha had defeated the other alii and had united the islands.

During Kamehameha's rule, the Kingdom of Hawaii began to trade with other countries. Workers cut down Hawaii's sandalwood forests and shipped the trees to China. The Chinese, who treasured the sweet-smelling wood, called Hawaii the land of "fragrant mountains."

A statue of Kamehameha I stands in Kapaau on Hawaii Island. Every year on June 11, flower necklaces called *leis* are placed on the statue to celebrate King Kamehameha Day.

Whalers hunted the giant sea animals for blubber, or fat, which was cooked to produce an oil that fueled lamps. Baleen, or whalebone, was used in making a variety of items, including fishing rods and umbrellas.

Hawaii also became an important rest stop for sailors from all over the world. Ships carrying furs from the United States to China anchored in Hawaii's waters. Whaling ships stopped in Hawaii for repairs and supplies. For many years, Hawaiians earned more money from providing whalers and traders with goods than from any other business.

These ships brought more than money and goods. The sailors carried diseases, such as measles and cholera, to Hawaii. Because the islanders had never been exposed to these illnesses, thousands of Hawaiians died.

More changes came to the islands after Kamehameha's son Liholiho became king of Hawaii in 1819. The new king ruled the islands with Kaahumanu, one of Kamehameha's wives. She persuaded Liholiho to end all kapu. This meant that Hawaiians no longer had to fear death for breaking rules. When the kapu ended, many islanders stopped worshipping Hawaiian gods.

At about the same time, outsiders came to teach Hawaiians a new religion—Christianity. In 1820 a group of **missionaries** from the United States landed on Hawaii Island. At first most Hawaiians did not like the new religion because of its strict rules. But after Kaahumanu adopted the missionaries' religion, many other Hawaiians also accepted Christianity.

The missionaries changed Hawaiian life in many ways. They created an alphabet so that Hawaiians could read and write the Hawaiian language. The missionaries opened schools and libraries and built hospitals and churches.

The Hawaiian Language

For hundreds of years, Hawaiians passed on their history and beliefs by singing special chants and telling stories aloud. No written language existed until American missionaries arrived in the early 1800s. The missionaries developed a 12-letter Hawaiian alphabet that included five vowels (a-e-i-o-u) and seven consonants (h-k-l-m-n-p-w). These letters matched the sounds of the spoken Hawaiian language.

Modern, written Hawaiian is very different from the original spoken language. Honolulu, for example, was probably once pronounced "Honoruru." But because the missionaries didn't always understand or respect the local pronunciation, they chose a spelling that matched what they thought they heard.

Nowadays people living in Hawaii use a few everyday Hawaiian phrases and words. But the only place where the language is commonly spoken is on the island of Niihau, which is inhabited primarily by native Hawaiians. A few older Hawaiians throughout the state still speak the language at home, and some churches offer services in Hawaiian.

aloha (ah-LOH-hah)	hello; good-bye
alohaaina (ah-LOH-hah-ah-EE-nah)	love of the land
haole (HOW-lee)	white person; mainlander
kupuna (koo-POO-nah)	grandparents
mahalo (mah-HAH-loh)	thank you
ohana (oh-HAHN-nah)	family
pau (PAH-oo)	finished; over

But the missionaries also banned many Hawaiian traditions, such as performing the *hula* dance and making colorful flower necklaces called *leis*. Hawaiians, who were used to wearing very little in the hot climate, were forced to wear heavy Western-style clothing. Those who became Christians could not smoke, drink liquor, fly kites, box, or wrestle.

In 1835 an American firm called Ladd and Company rented land on Kauai Island to start a sugarcane **plantation**. More of these large, privately owned farms were eventually established on other islands. In the next 40 years, sugar became the biggest industry in Hawaii.

The hula almost disappeared after missionaries banned the dance. But in the 1880s, King Kalakaua formed a hula troupe to revive the original dances, many of which are still performed today.

Plantation owners, most of whom came from the United States and Europe, hired Hawaiians to plant sugarcane, crush the stalks, and boil the juice that produced sugar. The sugar laborers worked 10-hour days, six days a week, for very low wages.

When Hawaiians refused to work under these conditions, planters brought in laborers from other countries. In exchange for their passage to Hawaii, the laborers signed contracts, agreeing to work on the sugar plantations for a certain number of years. They, too, worked long hours for low pay.

Hoping to earn more money than they could in their homelands, thousands of Chinese and Japanese **immigrants** came to Ha-

waii as sugar laborers in the mid-1800s. Smaller numbers of German, Portuguese, and Norwegian workers arrived later.

Some sugar laborers left Hawaii as soon as their contracts were over. But many of them stayed. They married Hawaiians and opened restaurants or small shops. By 1886 immigrants and people of mixed heritage outnumbered native Hawaiians.

The arrival of people from so many different cultures changed Hawaii. Asians built temples and shrines where they could practice their religions. Hawaiian, Japanese, Chinese, Portuguese, and English words mixed to form a new language—pidgin—that everyone could speak and understand.

White residents worried about the growing number of Asians in Hawaii. They were afraid that Asians might pass laws that white people would dislike. To prevent this from happening, several powerful white businesspeople tried to change Hawaii's government.

In 1887 these business owners pressured King Kalakaua to change Hawaii's election laws. Under the new rules, only men who owned $3,000 worth of land and earned at least $600 each year could vote. Sugar planters and other businessmen were the only voters who were that rich. They became the only people to elect government officials.

When King Kalakaua died in 1891, his sister, Liliuokalani, became the first queen of Hawaii. Liliuokalani wanted to stop the wealthy white business owners from having so much control over Hawaii. But in 1893, before she could make changes, a small group of planters and other businessmen overthrew the queen.

Most Hawaiians supported Liliuokalani. But they didn't have

enough soldiers or guns to fight the U.S. marines, who came ashore to help overthrow the queen. Liliuokalani's arrest ended the rule of kings and queens in Hawaii.

Liliuokalani *(above)* was Hawaii's first queen and last monarch, or royal leader. She was led to prison *(left)*, after trying unsuccessfully to take back control of her kingdom.

On August 12, 1898, a crowd gathered in Honolulu at Iolani Palace—the former Hawaiian royal residence—to watch the raising of the American flag. The event marked the formal annexation, or addition, of Hawaii to the United States.

After Liliuokalani was overthrown, Sanford Dole *(behind desk)* became the president of the new Republic of Hawaii. When Hawaii became a U.S. territory in 1900, Dole was appointed its first governor.

Sanford Dole, the son of U.S. missionaries, led Hawaii's new government. In 1898 Dole reached an agreement with the United States for **annexation** of Hawaii, making it a possession of the United States. On June 14, 1900, Hawaii became a U.S. territory. All islanders—except for Asians not born in Hawaii—became U.S. citizens.

Residents of the Territory of Hawaii paid taxes to the U.S. government, but they could not vote for president or for their own governor. To get these rights, Hawaii needed to become a state. But the U.S government refused to grant statehood to a territory like Hawaii, where less than half of the population was white.

In the late 1930s, war broke out in Europe and in Asia. The United States tried to stay out of the conflict. But on December 7, 1941, Japanese planes bombed the U.S. naval base at Pearl Harbor on the island of Oahu.

More than 2,400 of Hawaii's soldiers and residents died in the attack. The raiders destroyed almost 200 U.S. military airplanes and sank several warships. Angered by the attack, the United States declared war on Japan and joined World War II.

Fearing a Japanese invasion, the U.S. military immediately took over the Territory of Hawaii. For almost four years, the army controlled much of everyday life, from collecting trash to caring for the

...we here highly resolve that these dead shall not have died in vain...

REMEMBER DEC. 7th!

sick in hospitals to running Hawaii's courts of law. Thousands of U.S. soldiers and other military workers were stationed in Hawaii, and the territory's population nearly doubled.

Smoke and flames rise from an airfield *(above)* **after the Japanese attack on Pearl Harbor in 1941. Wartime posters** *(facing page)* **reminded Americans why the United States entered World War II.**

Senator Daniel K. Inouye, who served in the 442nd Regimental Combat Team during World War II, stands in front of a flag that carries the battalion's motto, "Go for Broke."

At the time of the Pearl Harbor attack, more than one-third of Hawaii's residents had Japanese ancestors. The U.S. government feared these people would spy for Japan or join a Japanese invasion of the islands. So the U.S. military arrested many Japanese Americans in Hawaii and closed Japanese schools and radio stations.

Although Japanese Americans were angered by these actions, they were determined to prove their loyalty to the country they considered home—the United States. The men in the 442nd Regimental Combat Team, most of whom were Japanese Americans from Hawaii, won more medals for bravery than any other battalion in World War II.

After the war ended in 1945, Hawaii was on its way to statehood. The government of Hawaii wrote a **constitution** (set of laws) that was approved by the territory's voters in 1950. The U.S. government could no longer refuse statehood, when the territory's people had shown heroism and great loyalty to the nation. On August 21, 1959, Hawaii became the 50th state.

The eight horizontal stripes on Hawaii's flag represent each of the state's main islands. In the upper left corner, a small version of Britain's flag honors British captain George Vancouver, who gave Hawaii its first flag in 1794.

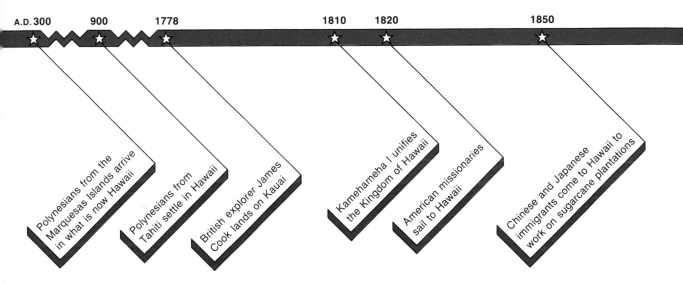

A.D. 300 — ★ — Polynesians from the Marquesas Islands arrive in what is now Hawaii

900 — ★ — Polynesians from Tahiti settle in Hawaii

1778 — ★ — British explorer James Cook lands on Kauai

1810 — ★ — Kamehameha I unifies the Kingdom of Hawaii

1820 — ★ — American missionaries sail to Hawaii

1850 — ★ — Chinese and Japanese immigrants come to Hawaii to work on sugarcane plantations

Hawaii has changed since it became a state. People of Hawaiian and Asian ancestry have gained some of the powers that Queen Liliuokalani wanted for them. The state's first U.S. representative, Daniel Inouye, is Japanese American. In 1985 the people of Hawaii elected the state's first native Hawaiian governor, John Waihee III.

But many Hawaiians are still angry that U.S. marines helped overthrow Liliuokalani 100 years ago. Some native Hawaiians want the islands to become an independent country once again. Others

40

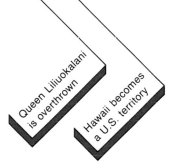

| 1893 | 1900 | 1941 | 1959 | 1985 | 1993 |

★ Queen Liliuokalani is overthrown

★ Hawaii becomes a U.S. territory

★ Japan bombs Pearl Harbor

★ Hawaii becomes the 50th state

★ John Waihee III is elected governor

★ Hawaiians mark the 100th anniversary of the wrongful overthrow of Liliuokalani

John Waihee III

want the U.S. government to recognize their status as a separate nation within the United States.

In the coming years, the state of Hawaii will look for ways to repay native Hawaiians for the country they lost when Liliuokalani was overthrown. At the same time, the state will continue to welcome the many groups of people who call the islands home.

41

Living and Working in Hawaii

In the Hawaiian language, the word *aloha* can mean "hello" or "good-bye." Aloha also expresses a feeling of affection or love for other people. Hawaii earned its nickname, the Aloha State, from this ancient tradition of friendliness.

Hawaii's hospitality, natural beauty, and warm climate have made tourism the state's most valuable industry. Each year the Aloha State welcomes about 6.5 million tourists, who spend a total of $11 billion during their stay. Most visitors come from the mainland United States or from Japan and other Asian countries.

Diamond Head on Oahu Island was named by British sailors who thought they'd discovered diamonds on the volcano's slopes.

Tour guides *(bottom, standing)* **and instructors** *(right)* **at the Polynesian Cultural Center on Oahu are among Hawaii's many service workers.**

44

The workers who help tourists in Hawaii have service jobs. These service workers include helicopter pilots who fly visitors over Hawaii's coastal beaches and lush, green valleys. Guides on Molokai Island lead trips on mules down the steep cliffs of Kalaupapa Trail. In Honolulu tour guides show visitors the Chinese temples and noodle factories of the city's Chinatown neighborhood.

Other service workers in Hawaii stock shelves in grocery stores, drive ambulances, or sell houses. Teachers, doctors, nurses, and members of the U.S. military also hold service jobs. Altogether, 87 percent of Hawaii's workers have service jobs helping other people or businesses.

Almost 19,000 of Hawaii's laborers—or about 6 percent of the workforce—earn a living from construction jobs. Some of these workers build hotels, stores, and restaurants in the state's cities and tourist areas.

About 65,000 people work for the U.S. military in Hawaii. Here, marines take part in a combat readiness exercise.

Only 3 percent of Hawaii's workers have agricultural jobs. Some farmers grow coffee, macadamia nuts, bananas, papayas, or avocados. Others raise hogs, chickens, or dairy cattle. Cowboys called paniolos raise beef cattle. Some growers cultivate orchids and other flowers, many of which are shipped overseas to be sold.

More than half of the money Hawaii earns from farming comes from sugarcane and pineapples, which grow only in tropical climates. Sugarcane plantations take up almost three-fourths of Hawaii's farmland. Most of the state's pineapples are raised on Maui and Lanai.

The pineapples and sugarcane grown in Hawaii are sent to the

Hawaii produces beef cattle (left) **and pineapples** (above).

state's factories, where about 4 percent of Hawaii's workers have jobs. Laborers in these factories slice and can pineapples and crush sugarcane for juice to make sugar. Other workers make bread, soft drinks, clothing, chemicals, and concrete. On Oahu, workers at oil refineries process petroleum that comes from Indonesia.

47

Hawaii's residents come from many different backgrounds.

Oahu is home to most of Hawaii's residents. Honolulu, the state's capital and largest city, sits on the southeastern corner of Oahu. One-third of Hawaii's 1.1 million people live in Honolulu.

Hawaii's other major cities are much smaller than Honolulu. Hilo, with nearly 38,000 residents, is located on Hawaii Island. Kailua, Kaneohe, and Waipahu—each with fewer than 37,000 people—are located on Oahu.

Many of Hawaii's residents, or their ancestors, came to the islands from other parts of the world.

Friends *(left)* **enjoy a day at the beach. A girl** *(right)* **performs a traditional Japanese festival dance.**

European Americans make up about 35 percent of the state's population. Another 25 percent are Japanese Americans. Native Hawaiians, whose Polynesian ancestors were the first settlers of Hawaii, make up about 15 percent of the state's residents.

Most of Hawaii's other residents have ancestors who came to the state from China, the Philippines, Korea, Samoa, and Southeast Asia. African Americans, American Indians, and Latinos make up only a small part of the state's population.

49

Nature's Necklace

When people arrive on or leave the Hawaiian Islands, they are usually presented with a lei. These beautiful flower necklaces are worn at many other occasions as well, including weddings and funerals. Historically, Hawaiians gave leis to their local alii, or chief, as a sign of affection. Warring chiefs who wanted to make peace sat down to weave a lei together.

Leis are made by stringing, sewing, or braiding together more than just flowers. Leaves, shells, nuts, seaweed, ferns, and other greenery are also commonly used. Each island has its own unique lei. For example, Hawaii's lei is made from the red *lehua* blossom, while Molokai's is fashioned from the green leaves and white flowers of the *kukui* tree.

Native Hawaiians are not the largest ethnic group in Hawaii, but their culture is an important part of Hawaiian life. Two well-known Hawaiian traditions are the hula, which means "dance" in the Hawaiian language, and the *luau,* a feast of Hawaiian food and dancing.

Many hula performers wear traditional skirts made from the leaves of *ti* plants. The dancers move their arms, hands, hips, and feet to a *mele,* or chant, that tells a story. Traditional Hawaiian musical instruments, such as the *pahu* (a large drum), accompany the dancers. At a luau, cooks roast a whole pig in an underground oven. Guests fill banana-leaf plates with pork, sweet potatoes, poi, and other Hawaiian foods.

The ocean is Hawaii's playground. Sailors glide from island to island with the trade winds. Below the water's surface, snorkelers and scuba divers can see a rainbow of colorful fish and more than 1,000 different kinds of glittering seashells. *Heenalu,* or wave sliding, is an ancient Hawaiian sport also known as surfing. Professional surfers ride the big waves each year at the Hawaii Pro Surfing Championships on Oahu.

On land, residents and visitors enjoy golf, tennis, hiking, horseback riding, and football. One of the state's best-known teams, the University of Hawaii's Rainbow Warriors, plays other college football teams from around the United States. A Rainbow Warrior might be selected to compete at the Hula Bowl, a college all-star football game held each January in Honolulu.

Hawaii's two national parks attract many visitors. At Haleakala National Park on Maui, adventurous hikers can walk into Haleakala Crater, an inactive volcano. The trail to the top of Mauna Loa at Hawaii Volcanoes National Park on Hawaii Island leads hikers past rare birds and hardened lava flows. From the Crater Rim Trail, which circles Kilauea volcano, visitors can look out over the volcano to see for themselves how Hawaii was born.

52

Cinder cones, formed from chunks of volcanic rock, rise as high as 600 feet (183 meters) in the crater of Haleakala volcano *(left)* on Maui. On Hawaii Island, fiery lava *(inset)* from Kilauea advances slowly across a roadway. Houses that lie in the path of a burning lava flow can catch fire.

When Polynesians first arrived in Hawaii, they discovered a richly forested land alive with honeycreepers *(inset)* **and other colorful birds.**

54

Protecting the Environment

When the Hawaiian Islands first appeared above the ocean millions of years ago, the land was bare. By the time the Polynesians arrived in Hawaii, at least 12,000 different kinds of plants, birds, and insects were living there! Most of these life-forms could be found nowhere else in the world.

Nowadays many of these unique plants and animals have become extinct. Of all the extinct plants and birds in the United States, nearly 75 percent were from the Hawaiian Islands.

Many of Hawaii's other species, or kinds, of plants and animals are also in danger of becoming extinct.

The state has more endangered birds than all of the other states combined, as well as almost half of the nation's endangered plants. How did all these plants and animals get to Hawaii? Why are they disappearing?

Over thousands of years, before the Polynesians discovered Hawaii, storms blew birds and bugs from Asia and other parts of the world to the islands. Some insects rode on drifting logs, while winds and ocean currents carried others. Seeds arrived on the feet or feathers of migrating birds. Seed-eating birds also left seeds behind in their guano, or droppings.

Palila and other types of Hawaiian honeycreepers live only in Hawaii.

Most of the seeds, birds, and insects that arrived in Hawaii were unable to survive. But every 30,000 years or so, a seed grew into a plant, which blossomed and produced more seeds. Birds or insects that survived the long voyage were sometimes able to find mates and to raise young. Scientists call the plants, birds, and insects that survived and reproduced pioneers.

Over thousands of years, the pioneers adapted, or changed, to continue to survive in Hawaii. But when Polynesians, Europeans, and other groups brought alien (new) plants and animals to the islands, Hawaii's life-forms were harmed.

For example, a flowering vine called the banana poka was brought to Hawaii from South America. Insects on that continent fed on the vine and kept its growth under control. But in Hawaii, where these vine-eating insects do not live, the banana poka grows out of control and has smothered more than 70,000 acres (28,350 hectares) of Hawaii's forestland.

Why Does It Matter?

Protecting Hawaii's plants and animals is important for practical, everyday reasons. Many of Hawaii's life-forms are valuable as medicines, for example. Found only in a few places in Hawaii, the *limu make o Hana* (a soft coral) is used to fight life-threatening tumors. To produce a type of cotton that resists insect pests, cotton breeders depend on a wild cotton found only in Hawaii.

Roots, mosses, ferns, and leaves in Hawaii's tropical rain forests trap most of the state's rainfall. The water filters slowly into the ground and fills up **aquifers,** or underground storehouses of fresh water, which are tapped to supply homes and businesses.

The survival of Hawaii's plants and animals is also vital to the culture of native Hawaiians. The state's plants provide materials for traditional Hawaiian clothing, ornaments, canoes, and medicines. Age-old songs, chants, and dances celebrate animals, plants, and natural sites.

Preserving Hawaii's variety of life-forms also protects the state's economy, which depends on a healthy environment to attract tourists. Thousands of visitors come to the islands each year to enjoy the state's lush plant life, colorful coral reefs, and clean beaches—as well as to see and learn about native Hawaiian traditions and culture. Steps taken today to protect the state's life-forms will add to Hawaii's quality of life for years to come.

Alien mammals such as pigs killed many of Hawaii's trees by digging up the roots and by eating the bark. Goats and cattle trampled or ate many native plants, which had not developed thorns, bad-tasting leaves, or other features to protect against grazing animals.

Mosquitoes, which came to Hawaii on trading ships in the 1800s, spread deadly diseases to Hawaii's birds. Dogs, mongooses, and rats attacked birds that built their nests on the ground. The mynah bird, which was brought to Hawaii from India in 1865, stole the nests of Hawaii's birds and competed with them for food.

Wild pigs *(left)* **can cause a lot of damage to their forest homes. Hawaii's forests are also threatened as workers cut down woodlands to make room for hotels, beach clubs, condominiums, and other buildings** *(facing page).*

The destruction of Hawaii's forests has also been deadly to the state's plants and animals. The early Polynesians burned down forests to create farmland. Over the years, farmers have continued to turn woodlands into cropland. Builders have cut down trees and filled in swamps and other wetlands to put up hotels and to create roads.

By 1992 nearly two-thirds of Hawaii's original forests, including almost half of the state's rain forests, were gone. Without the forests, many of the life-forms that depend on these areas for shelter and food cannot survive.

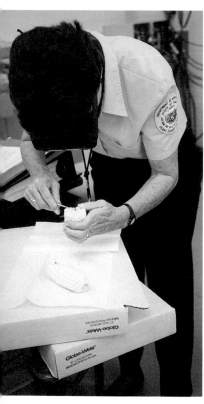

A government worker in Hawaii inspects corn for alien insects.

The people of Hawaii are striving to save endangered plants and animals. Scientists at the State Endangered Species Breeding Facility on Hawaii Island are working to raise families of endangered animals such as the *nene* (Hawaiian goose) and the *koloa* (Hawaiian duck). Researchers at botanical gardens are growing some of Hawaii's rarest plants, which will eventually be transplanted into areas where they cannot be disturbed by animals or people.

Hawaii has spent millions of dollars building fences to keep wild pigs and other alien species out of the state's forests. Environmental organizations are asking the government to prevent businesses from building in and polluting forests, wetlands, and other areas that are home to endangered plants and animals. Hawaii has also passed strict laws to keep people from bringing alien species into the state.

A tall fence at Haleakala National Park helps keep wild pigs out of the forest.

Hawaii's residents and visitors can help save the state's endangered plants and animals by leaving them alone. Pet owners are encouraged to keep their pets from running free so the animals can't eat or tear up native plants or kill Hawaii's birds.

The millions of people who visit Hawaii can help save endangered species by leaving their pets and any other alien animals or plants at home. Hikers from outside Hawaii can clean their boots to make sure their footgear doesn't spread alien seeds in Hawaii's forests. If everyone pitches in, Hawaii's wildlife has a chance to survive.

Hawaii's Famous People

MAMORU FUNAI

ARTISTS & WRITERS

Mamoru Funai (born 1932) writes and illustrates children's books. Among his award-winning books are *Moke and Poki in the Rain Forest* and *On a Picnic*. Funai is from Kauai.

Lois Lowry (born 1937), an award-winning children's book author, created the popular character Anastasia Krupnik. Lowry won a Newbery Medal in 1990 for *Number the Stars* and again in 1994 for *The Giver*. She is a native of Honolulu.

R. C. Leimana Pelton (born 1944) moved to Hawaii in 1980 to create sculptures from molten lava. He works near Hawaii Island's Kilauea volcano, shoveling lava into molds placed in trash cans, where the sculptures cool and harden. The finished pieces include abstract figures as well as vases and masks.

▲ **R. C. LEIMANA PELTON**

◀ **LOIS LOWRY**

◀ **AKEBONO**

ATHLETES & ASTRONAUT

Akebono (born 1970) is a 466-pound (211-kilogram) sumo wrestler. Born Chad Rowan in Waimanalo, Hawaii, Akebono moved to Japan in 1988 to learn the popular Japanese sport. Five years later, he became the first non-Japanese wrestler to rise to *yokozuna,* sumo's highest rank.

Charlie Hough (born 1948) is a pitcher from Honolulu. From 1982 through 1988, while playing for the Texas Rangers, he averaged 16 wins per season. A three-time World Series pitcher, Hough joined the Florida Marlins in 1993.

CHARLIE HOUGH ▶

Duke Paoa Kahanamoku (1890–1968) was a surfer who helped make the sport popular around the world. Also a champion swimmer, he won gold medals in the 100-meter freestyle event at the 1912 and 1920 Olympic Games. Kahanamoku was born in Honolulu.

Ellison Onizuka (1946–1986), born on Hawaii Island, was the first Japanese American to fly in space. He spent eight years with the U.S. Air Force before becoming an astronaut in the late 1970s. Onizuka was on board the space shuttle *Challenger* in 1986 when it exploded shortly after takeoff, killing all crew members.

▼ ELLISON ONIZUKA

▲ DUKE PAOA KAHANAMOKU

JAMES DOLE ▶

WILLIAM ▲ PATTERSON

WALTER ▶ LAPPERT

BUSINESS LEADERS

James Dole (1877–1958), the man behind Dole pineapple products, moved to Hawaii in 1899. He opened a cannery and begin shipping the first canned pineapple to the U.S. mainland. Dole's success encouraged others to grow the fruit, which became Hawaii's second largest industry.

Walter Lappert (born 1921), a businessman originally from Austria, retired to Kauai, where he opened an ice cream shop in 1983. Using Hawaiian ingredients such as guavas and mangoes to make unique flavors of ice cream, he turned a small store into a $15 million business.

William Patterson (1899–1980) built United Airlines into one of the world's largest commercial airlines. Under his leadership, the airline developed equipment that helped make flying safer and became one of the first to hire female flight attendants. Patterson was born in Honolulu.

63

Richard Smart (1913–1992), from Honolulu, ran the largest private cattle ranch in the United States. Parker Ranch, founded on Hawaii Island in 1847 by Smart's great-great-great-grandfather, produces about 10 million pounds (4.5 million kg) of beef each year.

ENTERTAINERS

Tia Carrere (born 1967) played Wayne's rock-star girlfriend in the movie *Wayne's World*. A native of Honolulu, Carrere released her first album, *Dream*, in 1993. She has also starred in the movies *Rising Sun*, *Wayne's World 2*, and *True Lies*.

Don Ho (born 1930) is a singer and nightclub entertainer from Honolulu. In the 1970s, he hosted "The Don Ho Show," a television program featuring music and songs from Hawaii. Ho is best known for his song "Tiny Bubbles."

◀ TIA CARRERE

◀ BETTE MIDLER

Bette Midler (born 1945) is an actress, singer, and Broadway performer. Raised in Honolulu, she has starred in several films, including *The Rose* and *Beaches*. Among her musical hits are the album *The Divine Miss M* and the song "Wind Beneath My Wings," both of which have won Grammy Awards.

NATIVE LEADERS

Kamehameha I (1758?–1819) became king of Hawaii in 1795. His family ruled the Kingdom of Hawaii until 1872, when Kamehameha V died, leaving no heirs. Kamehameha I was born in Kohala, Hawaii.

KAMEHAMEHA I ▶

Liliuokalani (1838–1917), Hawaii's last monarch, became queen in 1891 after the death of King Kalakaua, her brother. Liliuokalani tried to strengthen the power of the monarchy but was overthrown in 1893 by a small group of U.S. citizens. Born in Honolulu, she wrote "Aloha Oe," Hawaii's traditional song of farewell.

◀ LILIUOKALANI

POLITICIANS

George Ariyoshi (born 1926), governor of Hawaii from 1974 to 1986, was the first Japanese American to become a state governor. Raised in Honolulu, he was an interpreter for the U.S. Army during World War II. He later earned a law degree and served as a territorial representative and a state senator.

▲ GEORGE ARIYOSHI

◀ HIRAM FONG

Hiram Fong (born 1906) is a lawyer and businessman who became the first American of Chinese heritage to be elected to the U.S. Senate. The Honolulu native served three terms, which ran from 1959 to 1977.

◀ DANIEL K. INOUYE

Daniel K. Inouye (born 1924) was the first Japanese American to be elected to the U.S. Congress. After serving in World War II, he studied law and eventually entered politics. From Honolulu, Inouye was elected to the U.S. Senate in 1962.

Patsy Mink (born 1927), a lawyer and professor from Paia, Hawaii, was elected to the state senate in 1959. She went on to serve in the U.S. House of Representatives from 1965 to 1977, and in 1990 was reelected to the U.S. Congress.

PATSY MINK ▶

Facts-at-a-Glance

Nickname: Aloha State
Song: "Hawaii Ponoi" ("Hawaii's Own")
Motto: *Ua Mau Ke Ea O Ka Aina I Ka Pono* (The Life of the Land is Perpetuated in Righteousness)
Flower: hibiscus
Tree: kukui
Bird: nene (Hawaiian goose)

Population: 1,108,229*
Rank in population, nationwide: 41st
Area: 10,932 sq mi (28,314 sq km)
Rank in area, nationwide: 43rd
Date and ranking of statehood:
  August 21, 1959, the 50th state
Capital: Honolulu
Major cities (and populations*):
  Honolulu (365,272), Hilo (37,808), Kailua (36,818), Kaneohe (35,448), Waipahu (31,435)
U.S. senators: 2
U.S. representatives: 2
Electoral votes: 4

*1990 census

66

Places to visit: Akaka Falls State Park on Hawaii, Waimea Canyon State Park on Kauai, Shipwreck Beach on Lanai, Maui Plantation on Maui, Kalaupapa National Historical Park on Molokai, Bishop Museum on Oahu, USS *Arizona* Memorial on Oahu

Annual events: Hula Bowl on Oahu (Jan.); Narcissus Festival on Oahu (Jan./Feb.); Merrie Monarch Festival on Hawaii (April); 50th State Fair on Oahu (May-June); King Kamehameha Day on all the islands (June); Makawao Rodeo on Maui (July); International Festival of the Pacific on Hawaii (July); Hawaiian Pro Surfing Championships on Oahu (Nov./Dec.)

Natural resources: groundwater, titanium oxide, limestone, volcanic rock, forests, soil

Agricultural products: sugarcane, pineapples, beef and dairy cattle, eggs, hogs, flowers and leis, coffee, macadamia nuts, avocados, bananas, guavas, papayas

Manufactured goods: refined sugar, canned pineapple, bread, dairy products, soft drinks, newspapers, refined petroleum, clothing, chemicals, concrete

ENDANGERED SPECIES

Mammals—Hawaiian hoary bat, Hawaiian monk seal, blue whale, bowhead whale, finback whale, gray whale, humpback whale, right whale, sei whale, sperm whale

Birds—*akepa, akiapolaau,* Hawaiian coot, nene, koloa, crested honeycreeper, Maui parrotbill, Hawaiian petrel, Hawaiian hawk, Hawaiian stilt

Reptiles—hawksbill turtle, leatherback sea turtle

Plants—Mauna Kea silversword, Carter's panic-grass, hidden-petaled abutilon, *liliwai, alulu, awikiwiki, haha, nehe, loulu, opuhe, maua*

WHERE HAWAIIANS WORK
Services—68 percent
  (services includes jobs in trade; community, social, & personal services; finance, insurance, & real estate; transportation, communication, & utilities)
Government—19 percent
Construction—6 percent
Manufacturing—4 percent
Agriculture—3 percent

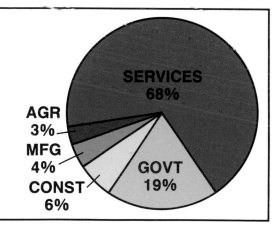

AGR 3%
MFG 4%
CONST 6%
SERVICES 68%
GOVT 19%

PRONUNCIATION GUIDE

Haleakala (hah-lee-ah-kuh-LAH)

Hawaii (huh-WAH-ee)

Hilo (HEE-loh)

Kahoolawe (kah-hoh-oh-LAH-vay)

Kailua (ky-LOO-uh)

Kamehameha
(kah-MAY-hah-MAY-hah)

Kaneohe (kah-nay-OH-hay)

Kauai (kow-WAH-ee)

Kilauea (kee-low-WAY-uh)

Lanai (lah-NAH-ee)

Liliuokalani
(lee-LEE-oo-oh-kuh-LAH-nee)

Maui (MOW-ee)

Mauna Kea; Mauna Loa
(mow-nuh KAY-uh; LOH-uh)

Molokai (moh-loh-KAH-ee)

Niihau (NEE-ee-HOW)

Oahu (oh-AH-hoo)

Waipahu (wy-PAH-hoo)

Glossary

annexation Adding a country or other territory to another country or state that is usually bigger and more powerful. Annexation can take place peacefully or by military force.

aquifer An underground layer of rock, sand, or gravel containing water that can be drawn out for use above ground.

constitution The system of basic laws or rules of a government, society, or organization. The document in which these laws or rules are written.

coral Rocklike formations made up of the skeletons of small sea animals called coral polyps. Coral is found in warm seas.

immigrant A person who moves into a foreign country and settles there.

lava Hot, melted rock that erupts from a volcano or from cracks in the earth's surface and that hardens as it cools.

missionary A person sent out by a religious group to spread its beliefs to other people.

plantation A large estate, usually in a warm climate, on which crops are grown by workers who live on the estate. In the past, plantation owners usually used slave labor.

plateau A large, relatively flat area that stands above the surrounding land.

tropical rain forest A dense woodland with large amounts of annual rainfall— at least 80 inches (203 cm), but often much more. These forests contain tall evergreen trees and many other plants and a wide variety of animals. Tropical rain forests are located in hot, wet climates near the equator.

Index ━━━━━

70

Acknowledgments:

Maryland Cartographics, Inc., pp. 2-3, 10-11; Buddy Mays / Travel Stock, pp. 2-3, 6, 14, 17 (inset), 29, 42-43, 44, 49 (left), 50, 52-53, 54, 71; Jack Lindstrom, p. 7; U.S. Geological Survey, p. 8; © 1995, John Penisten / Pacific Pictures, pp. 9, 13, 15, 19, 20, 25, 46, 47, 49, 53 (inset); Cory Williams, p. 12; U.S. Fish and Wildlife Service, p. 15 (inset); Kay Shaw Photography, pp. 16 (inset), 61; Jack Jeffrey, pp. 16-17, 54 (inset), 56, 58; Hawaii State Archives, pp. 18, 22, 24, 31, 33, 34, 35, 63 (top left, center), 64 (bottom right), 65 (top left); Library of Congress, pp. 23, 37; New Bedford Whaling Museum, p. 26; National Archives (neg. #761), p. 36; Senator Daniel Inouye's Office, pp. 38, 65 (bottom left); Governor's Office, pp. 41, 65 (top right); DoD Still Media Records Center, p. 45; Elaine Little / World Photo Images, p. 48; Dan Lerner, p. 59, 68; Hawaii Dept. of Agriculture, p. 60; Mamoru Funai, p. 62 (top left); R.C. Leimana Pelton, p. 62 (top right); Amanda Smith, p. 62 (center); Reuters / Bettmann, p. 62 (bottom left); Texas Rangers, p. 62 (bottom right); NASA, p. 63 (top right); United Airlines, p. 63 (bottom left); Lappert's Hawaii, p. 63 (bottom right); Parker Ranch, p. 64 (top right); Hollywood Book & Poster, p. 64 (top left, bottom left); U.S. Senate Republican Party Committee, p. 65 (center); Congresswoman Patsy Mink's Office, p. 65 (bottom right); Jean Matheny, p. 66.

DATE DUE
